HOW IT WORKS

Helicopters

by Kaitlyn Duling

BLASTOFF! 3 READERS

BELLWETHER MEDIA • MINNEAPOLIS, MN

Blastoff! Readers are carefully developed by literacy experts to build reading stamina and move students toward fluency by combining standards-based content with developmentally appropriate text.

 Level 1 provides the most support through repetition of high-frequency words, light text, predictable sentence patterns, and strong visual support.

 Level 2 offers early readers a bit more challenge through varied sentences, increased text load, and text-supportive special features.

 Level 3 advances early-fluent readers toward fluency through increased text load, less reliance on photos, advancing concepts, longer sentences, and more complex special features.

★ **Blastoff! Universe**

Reading Level

Grade **K**

Grades **1–3**

Grade **4**

This edition first published in 2023 by Bellwether Media, Inc.

No part of this publication may be reproduced in whole or in part without written permission of the publisher. For information regarding permission, write to Bellwether Media, Inc., Attention: Permissions Department, 6012 Blue Circle Drive, Minnetonka, MN 55343.

Library of Congress Cataloging-in-Publication Data

LC record for Helicopters available at: https://lccn.loc.gov/2022020067

Editor: Rachael Barnes   Series Design: Jeffrey Kollock   Book Designer: Josh Brink

Printed in the United States of America, North Mankato, MN.

Table of Contents

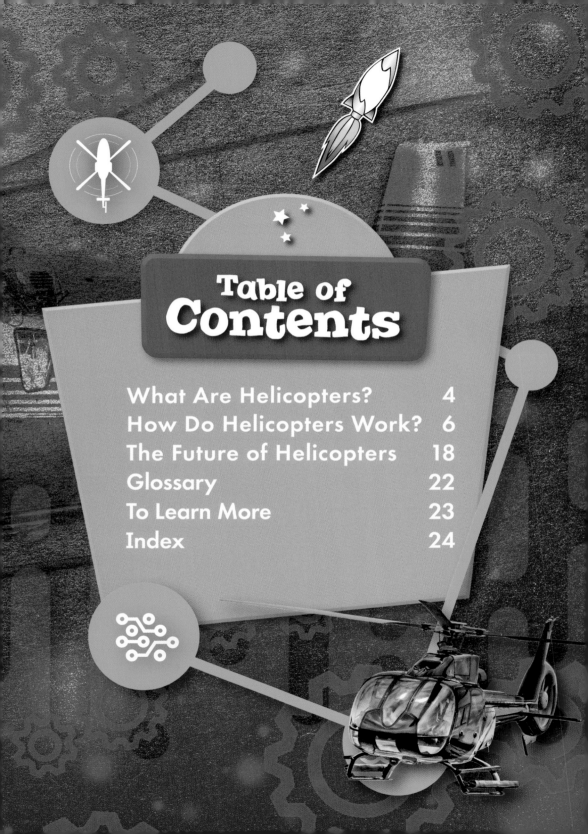

What Are Helicopters?

Helicopters are flying machines. Hospitals and militaries use them to carry people and supplies.

Firefighters use them to put out wildfires. People can take helicopter rides to see beautiful places.

military helicopter

4

main rotor

Helicopters are powered by an engine. It burns fuel to turn the **main rotor**.

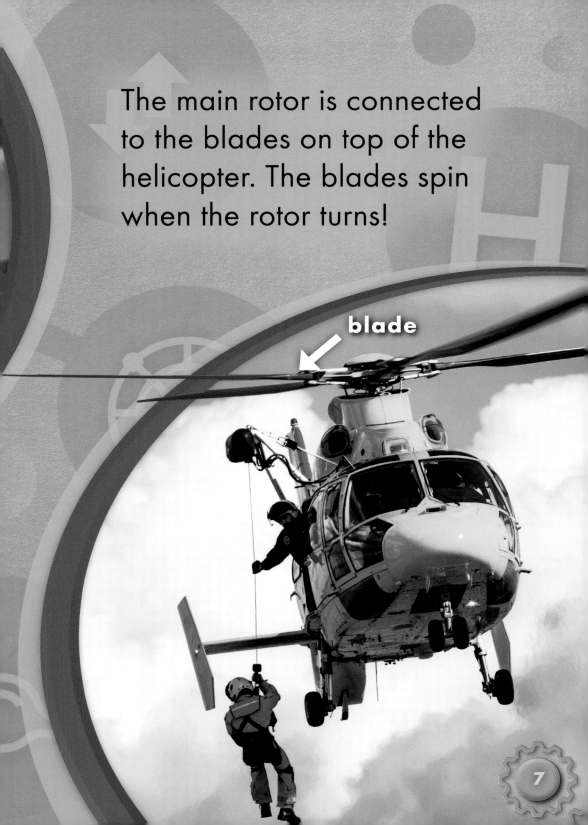

The main rotor is connected to the blades on top of the helicopter. The blades spin when the rotor turns!

blade

boom

tail
rotor

The spinning blades create **lift** and **thrust**. Lift helps the helicopter rise. Thrust can push it to fly in any direction.

The **tail rotor** spins blades at the end of the **boom**. This keeps the helicopter flying straight.

Parts of a Helicopter

main rotor

blade

tail rotor

engine

boom

cockpit

skid

nose

fuselage

A helicopter's weight must be spread out evenly from nose to boom. This helps it stay balanced while flying.

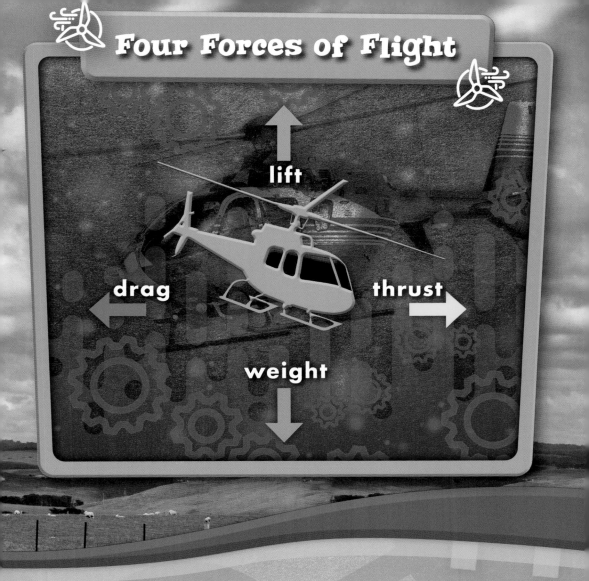

lift

drag

thrust

weight

Drag slows helicopters down. This force is caused by wind pushing against the **fuselage**.

cockpit

Pilots steer helicopters. They control all rotors from the **cockpit**.

Levers **tilt** the main rotor. This moves the helicopter in different directions. Helicopters can fly forward, backward, or sideways.

Flying a Helicopter

main rotor tilts forward

main rotor tilts backward

flies forward

flies backward

main rotor tilts left

main rotor tilts right

flies left

flies right

13

Pilots use foot pedals to move the tail rotor. The pedals change the direction the helicopter points.

foot pedals

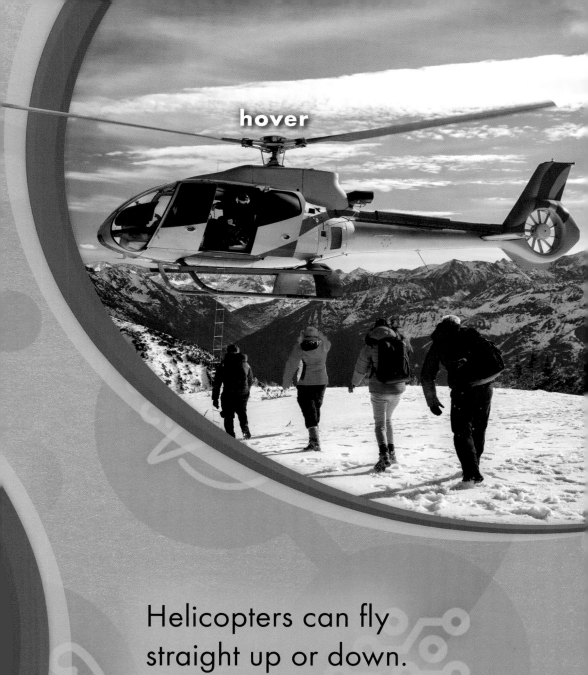

hover

Helicopters can fly
straight up or down.
They can even **hover**!

Helicopters have different tools to help them land. **Skids** are for landing on uneven ground.

Large helicopters have wheels to **taxi** after they land. A helicopter with **floats** can land safely on water!

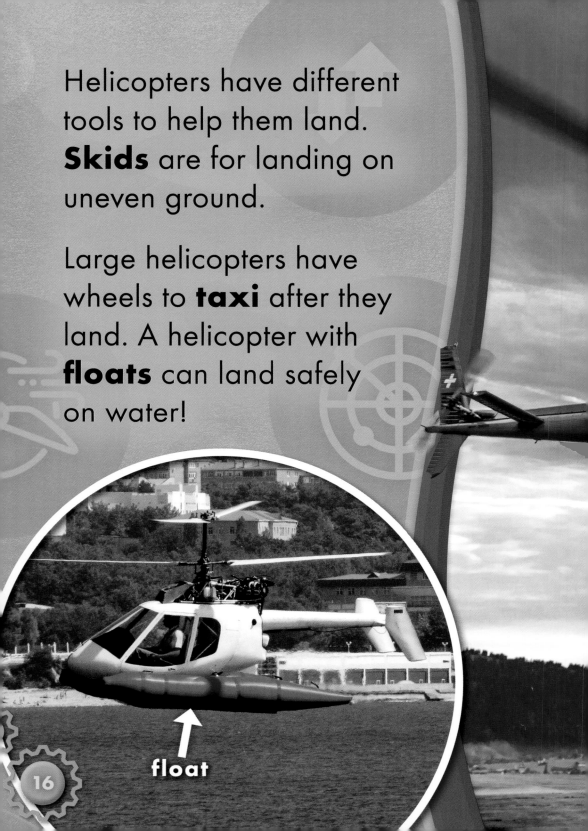

float

skids

The Future of Helicopters

Some helicopters have **dual rotors**. They are getting better every year!

These rotors help helicopters carry heavier loads. They will help future helicopters zip quickly and easily through unsafe areas.

dual rotors

Someday, helicopters may have four or more main rotors. They could easily fly through cities.

What do you think future helicopters will look like?

They could become part of everyday travel. These helicopters are going to wow the world!

Glossary

boom—the long, narrow back of a helicopter's body

cockpit—the part of a helicopter where the pilot steers

drag—a force that slows down motion

dual rotors—two main rotors, placed one above the other, on top of the body of a helicopter; dual rotors can also be called a coaxial rotor.

floats—inflatable skids used to land a helicopter on water

fuselage—the main body of a helicopter

hover—to remain in one place in the air

lift—a force that holds a helicopter in the air

main rotor—a device made up of many parts that connects the engine to the blades; the main rotor turns to give the helicopter lift and thrust.

skids—lightweight metal tubes on the bottom of a helicopter used for landing

tail rotor—a device with spinning blades located on the helicopter's tail

taxi—to drive a helicopter slowly on wheels along the ground

thrust—a force that pushes or drives something

tilt—to move to a new angle